HEPHZIBAH'S ANTHOLOGY

∽❧∼

Love letters between a lover of God &
the Lover of her soul

By

DAMMY FEYIDE

DEDICATION

To the King of my Heart.

You said to me,
'' Let it be known that I love you,
Let it be known of how much I love you,
Let it be known of how I love you,
Let it be known that you love Me too,
Let it be known that I have become your One Thing
Let it be known of how I became your One Thing."

I hope I have made You proud as I share of our love story. Thank
You for empowering and partnering with me on this.

CONTENTS

FOREWORD

⇛⇚

A lot can happen in a year:

You might wake up on the same bed for three hundred and sixty-five days in a row, but you won't always have the same thoughts, the same ideas about life or the same confidence in who you are – or, in who you always thought you were.

Somehow, when you look back at times past, you realise that there's been a slight shift – or, perhaps, several – in who you have become. You might look the same, sound the same, maybe even talk the same, but you can't always put your finger on all the many ways in which you are absolutely not the same.

The book you hold in your hands is a collection of faith-driven moments written over the course of a year that give expression to the subtle transitions that happen in our minds, our hearts and our souls even while our bodies continue to operate familiar routines. Dammy captures the shift that would otherwise have gone unnoticed, the questions we have as we grow in our faith and puts them within the framework of the Love of God, painting us little pictures of what God's heart looks like to those who believe – even if that belief is a faint, stumbling struggle to hold on; is tested through the uncertainties of time, and often seems impractical and undefined.

Hephzibah's Anthology documents Dammy's intimate questions and conversations with God in pieces, glimpses and moments. It is like an exotic box of chocolates, each piece having a unique filling that stirs you up on the inside to experience a different flavour of what life could be with God. And, like any box of chocolates, it is not to be rushed: savour every bite, every entry, every piece.

As you read, you will notice that Dammy stops to smell the
roses even when the thorns hurt and the petals wither. You might
feel a prick or two, yourself, as her journey bumps against your own
memories… and yet, there is healing in the process. Let her words
mix with your thoughts, the questions in your heart and your own
uncertainties. Sit with it, exploring every new emotion that each
entry stirs up, asking your own questions and finding a connection
with her process before moving on to the next.

Not everyone starts off understanding what the journey
with Jesus will look like. Not everyone is bold enough to admit
that they do not understand, and not everyone is strong enough to
continue to walk with Him even through the roughest patches to get
to a place where they can believe, regardless. I invite you to use this
anthology as a source of inspiration, a picture of what could be, as
you navigate your own unique and very personal journey with God.

Omotayo Adeola

Damilola typifies one who is in love with her Creator,
not without flaws however, and it is on that journey she invites us
on, in her relationship with God. She is bold in being vulnerable,
exposing not just her strengths but the entirety of her walk with
the Father. If you are seeking for greater intimacy with the Father,
I will recommend you read this. Often when we hear the story of
champions, we see how they rise but not when they falter, as few
people are bold enough to open the treasure chest which shows the
pain, disappointment, the joys, the highs and the lows. The highs are
equally as important as the lows, for in them we discover not only
who we are, but who God is.

One of the greatest lessons from the book is how much God
loves us and He is more real than the air we breathe. He is always
with us through pain, tears, joy, and success. He is a faithful Father

and when we don't feel or see Him, it isn't Him that has moved; it is
we that may have wandered away from His presence… you will find
that words of the Bible say it best in Isaiah 61:3, **"To appoint unto
them that mourn in Zion, to give unto them beauty for ashes,
the oil of joy for mourning, the garment of praise for the spirit
of heaviness; that they might be called trees of righteousness, the
planting of the LORD, that he might be glorified."**

This is premise of this book - that whatever your story is,
whatever you have gone or are still going through, God is an expert
in making your life truly beautiful. You will learn about your identity
and come into the fulness of who and what God has called you to be
without being ashamed. You will realise that the best place to be is to
be in God.

Pastor Afolabi Anibaba

INTRODUCTION

This is to you.

To you who is lost and has lost

To you who has decided to take this leap and is figuring out how and where you fit into this new.

To you whose perspective has changed.

To you whose whole world has changed, while everything still looks the same.

To you who is trying to make sense of it all.

To you who is willing but terrified of opening up your heart completely

To you who is wondering if you are alone in this.

To you who is hopeful.

To you who is trying to make sense of all the loss, of all the pain, of the trauma.

To you who now understands that there's a why.

To you who desires wholeness

To you who has encountered something bigger.

To you who is tired of running.

To you who is tired of battling living the best of both worlds.

To you who is ready to rediscover who you originally were meant to be.

To you who has a new desire.

To you who is shedding.

To you who is tired of the distorted reality and ready to accept the truth, the actual reality.

To you who is trying to understand how you can be so unworthy yet still so worthy of this kind of love.

This is to you.

I hope you can grow through all these day after day as you experience my journey with me. I hope it gives you hope, I hope it empowers you, I hope you see that despite it all, God does not play when it comes to His own. I hope you understand that it is not easy to walk with Him and that it will cost you but it is the most satisfying and indeed the best thing you will ever do.

As you will come to read and realise, I hope that like me who has lost and been broken, you will understand that restoration is possible. True love, true friendship, true partnership, true father-daughter love, true purpose, true acceptance, true purpose, true validation and the only one that matters is an inheritance and nothing you will ever deserve or need to work for in Christ.

I hope you can relate, see yourself and struggles in me and know that as I laid it as His feet so can you. It is only thereafter that you can also overcome and go into a place of deeper, and of greater.

REQUEST BY THE AUTHOR

Dear Reader,

I really hope you can take me at my word and grant me this one request as you embark on the journey that is this book.

I ask that you take your time, that you take a day or two after going some chapters in, drop this book and mull over it for a little while before moving forward. This body of work is a collection of conversations between myself & my Father.

So, I really ask that you also go on this journey with me whilst you get out of it whatever it is that you do just like I did.

Thank you,
D.

PREFACE

For a while there, I thought I lost You. You weren't my first love; You weren't my love at all if I am honest, but today I sit reflecting and grateful for the journey. You know, people have come and gone; hobbies, desires, and interests have grown and waned… things have happened but You remained steady and patient (I DO NOT KNOW HOW). You were like that boy that never got the hint, persistently chasing, even in times when You were just my rebound, in the times when it was just a seasonal kind of love, in challenging times, times when I just wanted something so bad that I enjoyed and seemed open to the chase, You remained faithful.

Today, I sit in the same place where You ignited a fire in a part of me that burned out, but what You did was to give it new meaning, new life, and purpose. You took me back to what you originally created it to be and it means something special now. It is so different from what I wanted it to be as a young girl who had a passion for putting pen to paper. You have disrupted what I planned for it to be so it can become what it was meant to be. You have made it better, and it's no longer just my thing but Our thing. This is what they call a full circle moment. I always say I am glad and grateful for your corny, funny yet not-so-funny ability to bring it all together and this is no different. Now if they ask me what I do or what I am good at, my response is, I write on Purpose.

28th September 2019

*At the Chara Unlikely Vessels Event
Maz said something to me that made me think, "Wow! God, look at our
journey. This alone is a testimony."*

EMBRACE

৵৽

The moment you stop running,
You make it a little easier for the chaser,
To catch you,
To break down walls,
To heal,
To dwell,
To work,

To walk,
To love,
To hold you,
To embrace.
All of a sudden,
You are caught,

You are broken,
You are healing,
You are dwelling
You are letting work be done,
You are being used,

You know now what it means to be loved,
You are loving just right back,
You are understanding,
You see clearer.

Then you start to wonder, why was I running?
Is this what it feels like?
Such wasted time,
Wasted years,
Wasted energy,
Wasted tears.
So now you protect,
You chase after right back,
You seek,
You begin to experience a new season

Of unending love,
Of joy,
Of grace,
Of peace unlike anything you have ever known,
Of understanding,
Of faithfulness,
Of enlightenment,
Of a new and true relationship,
Of a new level of intimacy,
Of partnership,
Of hearing and listening,
Of obedience,
Of boldness,
Of unmerited kindness,
Of patience,

Of mercy,
Of convictions,
Of a new perspective,
Of loving,
Of a new reality,
Of identity,
Of a new kind of battle,
Of understanding you have been predestined,
Of knowing there is more,
Of more,
Of life…
It is a new season.

7th October 2019

In the office {"You take what the enemy meant for evil and you turn it for good" by Hillsong}

VICTORY

৵৶

How can we have experienced this or know this and not have a new perspective followed by a new response going forward? Seems almost disappointing and insulting for our responses to be so doubtful, fearful, full of anxiety, worrisome, after we have experienced You, but let me not get ahead of myself. Back to my point…

So, you mean me not getting that job,

That toxicity and attack of that relationship, The big relocation,

Being fired from the last job,

Flunking out of the program or school,

That business failing,

The periods of being molested,

The heartbreaks from my earthly hero,

Being the odd man out,

Always feeling out of place and uncomfortable,

No one understanding,

Those isolated moments,

The distractions,

The anxiety,

All the pain,

All the loss,

All the failures,

The influences,

The abuse I suffered,

That unhealthy relationship that was a spiritual attack,
Me looking for love in the wrong places, the broken places,
Hitting rock bottom to the point of numbness and brokenness
...all the things meant to distract and then attack until they killed me.
You mean they were meant to happen? And the ones that were not meant to but did, You mean those were still okay?
You are all-knowing, Omniscient God. So, that tells me You already took account of all these things.

While I cried, while pieces of me kept being taken away, while I was floating and then breaking, while that hurt You because of how much You love me and hated to see me that way, it means You smiled and wished I smiled through them too. You smiled and wanted me to smile because You already knew the plans You had for me and how all these things were for a reason that You knew was needed. I just could not see it or see past what was my reality and so my response was not a smile or even worship to be honest.

Makes me wonder, do You just wait till we get to that 'Aha' moment while just marveling at how slow we are to understand when we finally get there? How do You not get frustrated with us, honestly? I would be but that is why You are You, I guess.

How silly we are, not realizing that when the time came, we would laugh and respond differently with stories of how it all worked out because it did all work out and even better than how we wanted it initially…. as it was meant to.

We say we trust You, but then why isn't our response like that of Job in the Bible, like that of someone who trusts You?

Why are there a million burning questions, doubts, anxieties, tears of sadness, demoralizing thoughts, and declarations of failure? Why does the worship stop? Why do we get disappointed and give up?

My friend Mirabel once said to me, "He has the devil on a leash" and I laughed so hard but felt so comforted at the same time. So, maybe this is what needs to be experienced and remembered about You. Then, we can really trust you, because how can my response not be power or faith or boldness when my Father has my adversary on a leash?

Then my response,
It will no longer be fear,
It will no longer be anxiety,
It will no longer be sadness,
It will no longer be on second thought,
It will no longer be overwhelming,
It will no longer be pain,

My response,
It will be faith and that faith will be activated by actions,
It will be of sound mind,
It will be peace amid chaos,
It will no longer be shaken,
It will be joy,
It will be praise,
It will be worship,
It will be victorious,
It will be You, My Source, My Vine.

10th October 2019

Thursday alone time before TTWJ starts. I call it 'The Calm' {"When you are finished, I am so much more"- Good & Loved by Travis and Steffany}

HE IS SO MUCH MORE
HE HAS SO MUCH MORE

೩∼৩

Not too long ago, I hit rock bottom, the lowest of the lows. Honestly, nothing worse could have happened as far as I was concerned, and my heart was shattered. Brokenness felt like my middle name, I was always just waiting on the next hit. Little did I know that He does His best work in a place of brokenness.

"Surrender, surrender", it seemed to be the theme and headline as I entered this new territory. When I thought I had surrendered, I quickly learnt there was more. So, I had to keep digging for I had touched something. Then, I hit something and I thought I was finished.

How can anyone come back from this, where to start from?
It is deep
It is not a quick fix
It is filled with generational entanglement
It is sick
It is vile
It is toxic
It is messy
And it hurts.

There is real pain and so much healing to be done. This had been 25 years, at this point it seemed like it was over.

Only at the point of complete surrender, invitation, intimacy, brokenness did the healing journey truly begin. It was time to bid farewell to a lot of things and prepare for something beautiful that was beginning with me and the time was here.

I said I was finished and felt complete emptiness for the first time at that moment. I literally had nothing left to do, my only resort was Him so I let Him in.

He has shown me love

He is healing

He is teaching me obedience

He has liberated me

He is showing me how faithful he is

He has given me grace

He is helping me exercise faith

He is letting me dream again

He is reintroducing me to old gifts and interests

He is using me

He is filling me up with peace

He is replacing the bad with good

He is restoring

He is making me rest

He is teaching me to walk not run, to stride and not to strive

He is showing me I need not to ever struggle

He is showing me I am the exception

He is teaching me that things follow me and I do not need to chase after them

He is allowing me experience unlimited favor

He has given me authority

He is making me bold

He is pushing me out, no more room for hiding

He is opening my heart

He is filling me with new ideas
He is giving me vision
He is teaching
He is helping
He is dwelling
He is giving to me a father's love
He has given me joy
He has given me newness of life
He is helping me live my best life, my best God life.

When I thought I was finished, and it was all over, **He said "No. Now, you can finally start living. With Me, there is life and life abundantly. Once you invite Me to walk with you, you will understand that what you were doing is nothing in comparison. Just come to me, I have so much for you; I have abundance for you; I have a plan for you; I have a reason for you; I have gifts for you; I have joy for you; I have peace for you; I have freedom for you; I have power for you; I have strength for you; I have an inheritance for you; I have healing for you; I have love for you; I have Me for you; I have Life for you."**

15th October 2019

In the office

TO DIE

To die to self,
Is crucifixion.
To die to self,
Is trading worldliness and flesh for the spirit.
It is to have no control.
To die to self,
Is to no longer be at the centre,
It is to know it is not about you.
To die to self,
Is to no longer conform to the ways of the world,
It is to be transformed.
To die to self,
Is to know there is a plan,
It is to know however that it is not yours.
To die to self,
Is to know your story is not your story and never was
It is His story.

To die to self,
Is to surrender,
It is having no control and it is selflessness.
To die to self,
Is humility,
It is courage.

To die to self,
Is to be vulnerable to persecution,
It is accepting persecution & the misunderstandings of your actions.
To die to self,
Is shedding
It is losing.
To die to self,
Is taking accountability,
It is sacrifice.
To die to self,
Is to lay down your rod
It is to take up His rod instead.

To die to self,
Is to not know,
It is to not understand,
It is to keep going when it you cannot see it
It is to keep going when you cannot feel it.
To die to self,
Is to take up your cross,
It is to follow.
To die to self,
Is patience
It means trusting,
It is peace knowing you trust.
To die to self,
Is receiving His salvation and all that comes with it
Freedom, Faith, Grace, Favour, Unconditional love.

To die to self,
Is availability to be used,

It is to be a vessel.
To die to self,
Is to allow His gifts to be manifested through you.
To die to self,
Is to not have a backup plan.
To die to self,
Is spirit over flesh and earthly desires.
To die to self,
Is to be a student and follower forever,
It is grace to remain in a place of continuous wonder.
To die to self,
Is to no longer be conformed to the world,
It is to no longer let the voices, define and lead you.
To die to self,
Is to be transformed by a renewal of the mind.
To die to self,
Is to be reborn.
To die to self,
It is to let work be done through you.
To die to self,
Is stewardship.
To die to self,
Is to know you are & can do nothing without He who is your source.
To die to self,
Is to seek to stay connected to the Vine at all costs.
To die to self,
Is to bear fruit, fruit that lasts.
To die to self,
Is to know whose you are.
To die to self,
Is to no longer live this world or anything in it.

To die to self,
Is to walk like Him,
It is to walk with Him,
It is to work for Him,
It is to play your part,
It is to live the life He has called you to live.
To die to self,
Is to be in the world but not of the world.

22nd September 2019

At Nuli for exam prep.
Reviewing people's prayer requests which they had sent to me at my request.
A lot of people are asking about purpose.

ON THE FAMOUS QUESTION

❧

Do not get fixated on figuring out your purpose that you are no longer able to read between the lines or pay attention to what is happening to you right now.
Your purpose could be manifesting right in front of you. Even if that's not the case, focus your prayers on the important thing, on the One who gives purpose. How is your relationship with Him?

If He does reveal the purpose we are after, do we have enough faith to humble ourselves at this very moment to be obedient to the call? Do we have wisdom enough at this moment that is required for the said purpose, are we ready? Are we mature enough? Have we given Him complete access to our lives, where there is no area that is no longer hidden, are we still hiding or running? Have we identified that healing is necessary? Have we turned away from our own self-righteousness and legalism? Have we made ourselves available to be used? One of my favourite pastors, Michael Todd once said, 'He cannot help what you are pretending to be, only what you are.'

Ephesians 2 says "before we were born, He predestined us". We, as members of His household, are all being built together for a dwelling place of God in the Spirit. This means that we all have a purpose, but all He has asked is for us to seek Him and only Him and He has promised that the rest will follow. He's asking that we do not worry about what's ahead but instead, enjoy and pay attention to every step of the journey as we fix our eyes on Him. In turning your attention to what He is currently doing, you will find that it will all align and begin to manifest in your life. So, now if anything, let us pray for guidance, and for direction to keep us in line with whatever He has for us as we keep our eyes and heart set on Him alone.

Our desire to know and have 'purpose' revealed to us could become a form of pride that we need to constantly check. Think about it - why do we want to know what our purpose is so badly? Is it so we can add our own suggestions or interpretations or begin to strive and then take control on how we get there? Is it so we can somehow drive it, work for it, plan for it, till it becomes our thing and take away His glory? Some will say, "it is the control freak or the planner in me" but is that not pride?

We cannot get away from the word "surrender" because the truth is, it was and will never be about us in the first place. It is His Story. **Sometimes, surrender also means not knowing and being okay with that.**

22nd October 2019

In the office

TRUTH IS WE CAN ALL BE MARTHA

It is so funny that when we first heard the story of Jesus' visit with Mary and Martha, some of us (me included) were so quick to either point accusing fingers at Martha or not want to be like her following the lesson.

Truth is, we have all been Martha or come close to being like her, especially for those of us who are in positions of service in one way or another. Service to God I say, exposes that blurred line of the distractions in the line of service. We experience Him so that our eyes are fixed on Him and want more, and we develop growing intimacy in our relationship with Him. That intimacy involves hearing from Him and keeping a communication line. He asks from us and leads us to abide in Him, we obey and what a privilege to be entrusted with such gifts, tasks from Him, for Him, for His glory through us. In our obedience to do these things, often without us realising it becomes all consuming, or in some cases, no longer about Him. It then becomes about us, how we feel, or the glory we're receiving. Sometimes, we so forget Who sent us that we take charge and become the boss with even our prayers and intimate time with Him becoming about the thing and no longer about the One who should matter above all else.

You begin to ask:
- What word do you have for me for this person or this group?
- How should today's event/session/class/preaching/worship go?
- What structure seems good?
- What am I supposed to do with this?

- Who should come speak?
- Where do we go next?

You begin to experience the following:
- You cannot worship or hear a new song and not be thinking about your worship playlist for an event
- It becomes from gift of administration to control freak and planner
- It becomes your thing and not His thing
- You pray more about receiving a word or guidance about the thing than just worshipping or spending time talking intimately with Him

These and so much more become our thoughts, our heart desires and then our heart's treasure, taking His place. We end up coming to Him because of the thing He has asked us to do, forgetting that it was Him that give it to us in the first place forgetting. The most underestimated and dangerous realisation is that we can serve God in our rightful place but be so distant from Him, by being so consumed with the assignment that the intimacy is lost.

Martha should not be someone we run from or ever condemn. She should be someone we learn from instead and should serve as a constant reminder and a guide. Distractions will come in various forms; even good things could be distractions. My friend Maz once told me about how my worship sessions were a distraction and my escape from intimacy with Him as I tried to avoid any moment of silence where it was just Him and I and she was right. Imagine if this was true for worship sessions, how much so other 'good' activities?

Even in the things He has called us to do and gifted us with, we need to be careful. **What is my list of activities daily and how do they reflect what takes priority in my life? Food for thought.**

Martha was serving God in her own way by preparing a meal for him but she missed it still because that act of service consumed her more than simply sitting and waiting at His feet- the secret place, that is how easy it is for any of us to miss it, to be distracted. Mary kept her position at His feet, to take in His every word, and to abide in Him despite the ways she could have easily said she could serve Him. Staying forever at His feet is where He wants us to be, and that is where we should always be.

Do not get carried away by the works, the routine, the planning, the process, the gifts, the serving and their challenges so you don't get tired to the point of exhaustion. Remain and you will be fed, just as you are and use Martha as a heart posture check.

30th October 2019

Maz's guest room after reading the Masterlife Week 2, Day 5 material

RESTORER OF MY SOUL!

❁

I had to read John 15 for maybe the second time in my Masterlife discipleship exercise to look for what You were trying to say to me about remaining in Your word. Honestly, I was worried because I had read and meditated on this not too long ago, so I just kept wondering if you could possibly have anything new to say or point out to me about this scripture. My first mistake: I keep forgetting to stop boxing you and your ways and to take off every limitation.

As I read verses 2 to 5, I realised how incredible you are, as the words seemed completely brand new to me. It was as though this was my first time of seeing them. As I kept meditating on those verses that stood out, there was no need to have moved past to the other verses.

Verse 2 says, **"Every branch in Me that does not bear fruit He takes away; and every branch that bears fruit He prunes, that it may bear more fruit".**

Wow! This verse is just me and the way You are showing Yourself to me in this season, as my Restorer. You have been and still are revealing influences, habits, personality traits, and people to me that are not of You for me, even those that are good for me and are keeping me from bearing fruit like You have asked. You have been revealing things and tearing them apart - even the things that are good but not You. You are breaking me down to break me away from these things to be rebuilt. We have been having conversations about how I am becoming boring or rather, how my life is becoming boring in this weaning period. *Loooooool* I am aware it is not boredom. I am becoming different because I know different, and I see differently now. I see the fruitlessness of the former things and you are taking them away as you do your unveiling, so yes there is a gap in the transfiguration process but you've gone on to say that you are just pruning the branches that bear fruit so they can bear much fruit. You are doing that by healing and restoring.

You are restoring old interests and talents, restoring and giving new life to old and new friendships. You are replacing old things with new; that is why there is more of writing, talking, and teaching. Some relationships will not make it because maybe there is no fruit there, but You are replacing them with new ones. I see Your hands in that, to allow for fruit bearing, new interests and work that now replaces the void of the old, lifeless ones.

writing, fitness, music, Masterlife, ignite, career, families, TTWJ, skills, partnerships, events, teaching, friendships & relationships, sisterhood.

You do not leave to barrenness neither do you work incompletely; you restore to replace and heal what was lost but with even more.

In verse 4, You give the only prerequisite for restoration: **"Abide in me and I in you. As the branch cannot bear fruit for itself, unless it abides in the vine, neither can you, unless you abide in me".**

How crazy is it that as I read this over and over and picked up my pen to start writing this, the song "What can I do" by Tye Tribbett came on? I can't get over how intentional You are…

Honestly, where is the lie in this though? You literally say it yourself, **"for without me you can do nothing."** It's scary and comforting at the same time.

You are the God of Restoration, but to be restored, we need to remain.

Restoration can only happen when we remain, in You, in Your love, in our every word, so in the hearing, in the quiet, in obedience, in the teachings, in the seeking, in the receiving, in understanding, in the midst of the fire, in the light, in the source, in the vine.

For without Me, you can do nothing.

30th October 2019

Weekly Masterlife class talking about day 1 or 2

THANK YOU FOR FREEDOM

∾

To be liberated
Is to be set free
That comes from being reborn
From dying to self, to flesh, to culture, to the world and
That only comes from really knowing the truth which sets you free
(John 8:31-32)
The truth of who you really are, not how you see yourself or how the
world sees you but how He who you created sees you.
Do you know what it is like to be free?
To no longer be bound by the lifestyle,
To no longer be bound by the past,
By the experiences,
By the family ties and generational entanglement,
By the lies and opinions,
By culture,
By those who have hurt you,
By the influences.
To no longer be dead but to be reborn into a new reality by a new
perspective,
To be set free by new revelations,
To have brand new vision,
To stand in a place you were so used to, except it feels so different
while you are still looking the same, but the difference is that you are
seeing differently.

To stand unafraid,

To stand joyful, no longer dwelling on what used to be but grateful for new sight

Grateful for understanding,

Grateful for truth,

Grateful for His word,

Grateful for your identity in Him which simplifies it all,

Grateful for the experiences,

Grateful for His grace that covered and protected the worst that could have been.

To be liberated,

Is to understand salvation,

It is to receive salvation and all that comes with it; the unconditional love, immense mercy, unmerited grace and kindness, unending favour and faith.

This new stance, this new sight, this new joy, this new peace, this boldness is new life in freedom and in truth.

1st November 2019

{At work. Quiet time listening to "See a Victory" by Elevation Worship}

It is not and never was our battle.

This is why we are to worship our way through the battle we face because You have already won every battle, and so we've already won too. As your children, we are champions because You are the Champion. If this doesn't liberate you, bring you endless joy, a new level of boldness or unexplainable peace, then I honestly do not know what ever will.

Now I understand why there are some people, who are so fearless, full of joy, so at peace, and so unshaken. They know freedom because they know the truth which has set them free and they have chosen to walk and live in this newness of truth. This is why they walk differently.

So, their declarations,

Their courage,

Their calmness,

Their response,

Their faith,

Their moves, oh how they make moves, and how things move for them.

They are not misled or abnormal; they are walking with the truth that You have won every battle for them already and all they need to do is remain in You. They are aware of the truth that they no longer need to chase destiny, favour, opportunities, validation, love, good health, success, or open doors but that these things and so much more will follow them.

They live out of freedom, out of the love you have for them, out of the inheritance you have for them, out of the miracles you have made available for them, out of faith that you have given them, out of a revelation of who they are in You.

Thank you, thank you, thank you, for I will be them and even more.

5th November 2019

ABIDE

❧

Remaining and staying at Your feet means that I am not going to worry. I'm going to stay here and worship at Your feet and not be afraid or distracted by all that's going on. I am going to do all I can by Your strength to keep my position at Your feet.

The adversary will want me to get up and move from my position so he will continue to give me things to worry about, to over analyse till I can only see the bad, to attempt to control, to compare, to be upset about, to find offensive, to be prideful about, to be frustrated with, to build back up those walls you have tumbled down, to distract me until I have moved without even knowing it.

As much as you do not want to lose Me, I do not want to lose you and even more, that is why I keep chasing as The One. To keep reminding and showing you until you scale back, I keep convicting, I keep pushing you out to stop hiding and out of your comfort zone, I keep teaching to keep you growing so you understand the insignificance of the other things in comparison to Me. Remaining at My feet is just about abiding. What do you have outside of abiding in Me? Think of this whenever worry and doubt come or distractions set in and you will know.

In Me, you have truth, in Me you have light, in Me you have strength, and in Me, you have power. In Me, you have crazy faith. In Me, you have freedom. In Me, you have rest. In Me, you have peace. In Me, you have assurance. In Me, you have grace. In Me, you have been saved. In Me, you have been redeemed. In Me, you have been restored. In Me, you have complete healing. In Me, you have been validated. In Me, you have provision. In Me, you have comfort. In

Me, you have been delivered. In Me, you have gifts. In Me, they have been matured and manifested. In Me, you have a kingdom. In Me, you have abundance. In Me, you are fruitful. In Me, you are ahead. In Me, you bear lasting fruit. In Me, you have been accepted. In Me, you have everlasting joy. In Me, you have unconditional love. In Me, you have a purpose. In Me, you have life abundantly.

8th November 2019

{Day 2 Week 5. Looking through Masterlife at work. 1 Corinthians 12:31-32 and 13:13.}

LOVE

ঙ⌒ঙ

Love is the only thing that is perfect in His eyes. It's not about the works, the gifts, the acts of services or even the affirmations because without the fruit of love, it doesn't all matter. You can even do these other things so exceptionally but Psalm 139 is a heart cry out for Him to search us - **"Search me o God and know my heart, try me and know my anxieties and see if there is any wicked way in me."** He knows all things and, in the search, it's about whether these things are done from a place of love.

I am in constant awe of Your goodness because you have been so kind to give us a guideline on love - You have said we should love as You have loved us.

Hmmn… it's like a shiver just runs down my spine every time I hear that because I am reminded how much I am not able to love if we are going by Your standards and Your word or even by how much You have loved me.

Loving the way You love me is loving through pain and hurt.
It is loving patiently
It is loving even when they're undeserving
It is loving even when it's one-sided
It is loving despite
It is loving through the unknown
It is showing kindness even when I necessarily shouldn't given what has

transpired in the past
It is biting my tongue
It is not being too rash
It is loving even when you don't understand
It is forgiving no matter what
It is forgetting and not taking account
It is loving from afar in comparison to cutting off
It is loving past the insecurities
It is loving to surpass jealousy and fear
It is loving in the midst of the what ifs
It is sacrifice over and over again
It is honesty
It is loving without caution
It is dependent
It is accepting the pain that will come with it
It means understanding no one can be unworthy of love
It means 2nd, 3rd, 4th.... chances
It requires your strength.

This is what I take from this the most because I am still in awe of the mind blowing, reckless, unending, sacrificial, merciful, complete way You love me and show that You do; so that is how I know it will not be by my might to give that same kind of love to everyone.

So, help me God, equip me and fill me with Your love to exhale to others.

10th November 2019

{Quiet time before church}

GO IT ALONE

❧◈❧

This walk was never for you to go alone. I know you are used to going it alone, not letting people in to a certain degree, having gigantic walls up, having a third eye, always waiting for the other shoe to drop but that was in life without Me. Yes, you are right, you cannot depend on them neither should you put your trust in them. Trust Me. Trust in Me, and in My word, then you will trust in My plan, My body and all its members. 'Go it alone' ends here; there is no room for that in what I need you to do and be. This mindset no longer fits into this new life. So, go out, tell them, show them, hear from them, be there for them, put yourself out there for them, be vulnerable with them, teach them, give and pour out to them and take from them, learn from them and let them learn from you, no more running.

You are now part of a body and every part of this body is important as they are part of Me. I will give you the protection you need, I will equip you with all you need, I will increase your capacity, I will give you strength and at the same time I will protect your heart; so that even when the hurt and disappointments come, you are unshaken because you are not alone anymore. You now have Me;

To comfort you, to champion you, to protect you, to cover you, to heal you, to give you capacity, to defend you, to walk with you, to direct you, to give you wisdom, to be your strength, to be your light, to push you towards light.

From now on, you need not be afraid or practice severe self-preservation and protection. Go forth and love wholeheartedly, give wholeheartedly, obey wholeheartedly, do My work wholeheartedly. Do this by sharing, by welcoming, by joining, by being included and inclusive, by being all in, by being present, by building, by connecting, by witnessing, by bearing fruit, by sharing, by being an open book, by being who I have made you to be; all with open arms and by doing all things in love, no longer alone.

Wednesday 13th November 2019

"There is no greater feeling than being chased by The One!" - Me

THERE IS NO GREATER FEELING THAN BEING CHASED BY THE ONE- ME

ৡ৯

I said this a few weeks ago; I cannot remember within what context it was said (I have become a talker!) but I remember that I was with my bible study group and I had just read Ephesians 2. I am glad it meant a lot to those who heard me say it as it means everything to me, the one who has and continues to be chased by The One.

This world and the adversary will do everything in its power to dim your light, to the point that you lose that spring in your step born out of the realization of who you truly are and how you are special and chosen. Oh, and it is so easy to forget, to not feel special or chosen. What then happens is that your identity becomes hidden underneath all the other voices.

Today though, I have joy and I am filled with so much gratitude because You have reminded me what they have tried to make me forget, not see and understand. That You are my friend, and I am no longer a servant.

You did not choose Me, but I chose you.
You did not know Me first, but I knew you and I have always known you.
You did and do not know Me best, but I know you best.
You did not chase Me at first, but I did the chasing.
You love Me because I loved you first.
You did not appoint Me but I appointed you.

You did not save Me but I saved you.
You did not give Me a purpose but I made you for a purpose
You may not always keep chasing and seeking after Me, but I will
not stop going after you.

There is no greater feeling than understanding and knowing that I may be in this world but I am not of this world. That you have seen me, all of me - past, present, future, good, bad, ugly, vile, broken, healing, insecure, becoming- in every season. You have searched and seen me, yet You have still chosen me as Your friend.

You've chosen me to conform no longer but to stand out. To no longer live a life that pleases them or myself but one that pleases You. To take on persecution, hatred, isolation, judgment, condemnation, misunderstanding and trials. All because I am unable to conform because of what You call me, also knowing You went through these things and even worse - in that, I also find comfort.

Please help me to never get complacent, give me strength for when tiredness and dry bones and trials come, equip me with everything I need so I can be prepared, help me to never lose this friendship, help me against distractions and give me power over fear, teach me obedience to do all that You ask no matter what it is or what I may stand to lose. Show me that it is all nothing in comparison, so You can continue to trust me. I want to keep experiencing You in all Your beautiful limitless ways, to know You deeper, to become more of Your friend. I never want to go back to being a stranger, on the outside and a non-member of your household; I do not want to go back being dead and belonging to the world. I just want You and to dwell in Your kingdom so please help keep me here, never stop the chase, no matter how much I may push or how far away I may run.

25th November 2019.

{A day post-accident}

A NEW EXPERIENCE

You have given me a new testimony.

You have given me a new experience.

A new way to experience You, to know You, to encounter You, to call You a new name with all the conviction in the world.

You have added new meanings and stories to Your names. In the midst of the anxiety, the fear, the tiredness and the panic, there is truly only gratitude and praise. There is so much gratitude that I'm at a loss for words to express it; all I can do is worship, but I know You feel it, so that's okay.

You have shown me kindness and favour in a new way. You have shown me that You are always with me. I have seen Your grace and mercy and faithfulness and WOW! If there was ever a doubt that You are my friend, that You are my defender, that You are my father, that You are watching over me and with me, that You love me; then You outdid yourself in proving otherwise.

I remember calling out for You and shouting Your name as it was all happening all in front of me, as he lay on the ground bleeding from his head, unconscious. I remember it was all I could do, I just wanted to hand it over to You and at this moment, I am so grateful for the access to do so.

This experience has brought about fear, questions, anxiety, and robbed me of my peace and calmness. It has also left me feeling a bit off but as I worshipped because I couldn't do anything else, a line of song stood out to me: "because you are with me, I will not fear". A few days ago, on Friday to be exact, at the LYBL conference, You gave me a word, "STEP OUT". I wasn't too sure what it meant but as I sang those words over and over, I remembered Your word step out, and while I'm not sure what I'm stepping out of or into, yesterday made a bit more sense and I understand that the devil is going to try and take something away by filling me with fear. I'm smiling now because You have already given me Your word in 2 Timothy regarding the spirit You have given me which evaporates all fear.

So, I am going to step out in boldness even more, with the authority You have given me as I carry You on the inside of me. With more love, more compassion, more patience, more understanding, more peace of mind that surpasses worry, anxiety, sadness and loss, I am going to step out with You, stronger than ever.

28th November 2019

{In the car. On my way to Masterlife discipleship class}

"GET BACK IN THE RING"

જ્જ

Well, I know for a fact this isn't me...

In just meditating over 2Timothy 2, it just dawned on me that over the past week, I hadn't read and studied all that I had by accident. I see now how You were preparing me.

First, with 2 Timothy 1:7, my favourite....
Then 1 Timothy 6:12 again
Followed by James 1:2
And now 1Timothy 2:2

Until now, I didn't I realize I was in a battle, I mean of course I know, but this battle is different. You saying to me get back into the ring is not a small thing. I always say You're very funny, but this must top it. So, this is how you introduce me to the fight huh?

While getting back to the ring seems daunting and comforting at the same time, again You remind me of what a friend I have in You and most importantly, about my identity in You. You have hand selected and appointed me as Your friend, Your soldier, Your vessel and now more than ever, with the same things the devil tried to use to take me out, I feel more covered, more protected, more favored, more cherished, more empowered, more victorious, more of an overcomer, more grateful, more useful, more ready, more loved, more saved, more focused, more enlightened, more alert, more purposeful, more important, more joyful, more ready and more yours. More yours...and less like theirs as it was always meant to be.

4th December 2019

*{At discipleship class on presentation day, when asked how The Disciple's
Cross and Masterlife have impacted me so far.}*

GRATITUDE

❧

My response is different. This takes it back to us coming
weekly and fellowshipping together. From Mrs. F talking about road
rage, Brother S about not giving financially, and Mrs. J emphasizing
taking up the cross daily, these have been precious times.

I'm more intentional in loving
I'm more intentional in my response
-in showing kindness, selflessness, patience, taking up my cross.
I'm more intentional in letting go
I'm more intentional in opening up and opening up my heart
I'm more intentional in my learning as I learn
I'm more intentional in my sharing
I'm more intentional in my ministry
I'm more intentional in my growing
I'm more intentional in laying my cross at His feet
I'm more intentional in taking up His cross daily
I'm grateful for accountability
I'm grateful for new relationships
I'm grateful for communal nurture
I'm grateful for sharing and vulnerability
I'm grateful for the questions and confusion
I'm grateful for the answers and interpretations
I'm grateful for unlearning

I'm grateful for open hearts
I'm grateful for Miss A's always punctual tears
I'm grateful for growth
I'm grateful for the intentionality
I'm grateful for the light
I'm grateful for the stages and seasons
I'm grateful for the love in this room
I'm thankful for His presence
I'm grateful for the fun and banter
I'm grateful for this new family.

6th December 2019

{Started at work, ended at House of Prayer}

WHEN YOU MASTER YOUR EMOTIONS AND YOU DON'T LET THEM MASTER YOU.

❧◦❧

Today was hard,
Today was my own doing which is why it unfolded the way it did.
Today, learning and downloading happened albeit a painful one that resulted in a more painful consequence.

We talk about this disobedience thing and this thing of total surrender, but we need to dwell on the emotions that surround it and can lead you to a place of disobedience some more, so fewer people have to learn the painful way like I did.

Today, I found new meaning to the scripture "Guard your heart above all else" which is what the Holy Spirit impressed on me as I wandered around the office in my heartache. There are different interpretations of this scripture born out of different revelations and I am not a teacher trying to give it new meaning. However, this is what He said to me moments after this scripture came to mind, that gave it new meaning and life. When He says guard your heart, He is not only referring to the obvious things which is what we pay attention mostly to, but He refers also to the subtlety of the other things that can creep in and lead us astray.

We have underestimated our emotions; how vulnerable and human we are and how it affects how we begin to lead with our emotions or feelings rather than His words. The importance of protecting and mastering our emotions to the point where regardless of what feelings we are experiencing - fear, anxiety, pain, past experiences and projections, worldly desires, emotional needs - they are not enough reason to move against His words or instructions.

You know, just because it feels good or right does not mean it is Him or from Him. Just because it scares you, confuses you, or is uncomfortable, does not mean it is not Him either. Or what about when it is His promise but we have been instructed to hold on, but based off the enemy's secret weapon which is a 'hard press when we are in a tight spot', we move in haste before consulting Him instead of waiting on Him and His next word? Are we not single handedly self-sabotaging and forfeiting the promise?

Being the kind God that He is, He had warned us about our emotions and feelings, Paul in his letter to the Philippians (In Philippians 1:10, the Message version) said "You need to use your head and test your feelings so that your love is sincere and intelligent, not sentimental gush".

Now, do you understand that certain things that could have been avoided if you had meditated and understood this message earlier on? When Paul says, "so that your love is sincere", he is also talking about our actions. He is reminding us to not trust and act only based on sentiments but to test all feelings, where they come from, and what they are based on.

You let yourself become so emotional that you let your emotions lead you instead of Me leading you. You let fear lead you, you let your insecurities lead you, you let your lack of control over the situation overcome you, you allowed what seemed right and how you were feeling at that point lead you, such that it was no longer My word nor was I the center of the equation anymore. I ask you, was that because of what you deeply desire, fear, stubbornness, your human nature or just lack of trust in Me? As I am aware, it was not your intention to be disobedient as you did invite me to take charge initially. Nonetheless, you fell into disobedience, then I kept hinting at you to check yourself and what was taking My place as your heart's treasure because I could tell you were ignorant to the shift that was occurring but it did happen and you had to get to this point to understand why.

'He is still willing', my sister Tamara said to me, as I explained all that had happened and how bad I had messed up. Everything within me instantly seemed to quiet down, and shortly after that, I was just brought to tears. Amidst everything, in my disobedience, You are still so good; in my anxiety and haste, You are so pure and kind. Amidst my fears, You remain willing. You will teach, judge, convict, allow but You are still very much available and willing to fix, to heal, to save, to turn it around, to redeem, to fulfil the promise. It does not mean the promise changes, it may have now been delayed or forfeited because of my disobedience but Your promise is Your promise if we are able to recognize where we have gone wrong and come back to You.

9th or 10th Dec 2019

HE GIVES NEW NAMES

ॐ

John 1:42: ''You are Simon son of Jonah, you shall be called Cephas''. I read this and immediately noted, He gives new but the truest and most rightful names. There are so many more instances where He has specifically given new names in the Bible; Saul who then became known as Paul, Sarai who became Sarah, Abram who we now know as the father of multitudes Abraham, Jacob to Israel and so many others.

This new name goes back to our identity in Him and we do not even realise that while there are the more obvious and dramatic name changes, there are so many times He has called us new names too. While the world may have called us other things, most of them false and harsh, these tend to be the ones we hold onto and begin to find our identity in.

You might have been called - liar, barren, broke, sick, ugly, unintelligent, useless, failure, broken, addict, prostitute, murderer, slow, the one who got fired, the one who repeated class, orphan, jobless, angry, intolerable, single, sad, evil, a disappointment, dirty, abused, abuser…but He once said to me, **"Dammy, for every one bad thing he says about you, remember I have called you a thousand greater things."**

I sit now and can boldly say that He truly has time after time and from that moment on, His word has become my default refuge whenever I am called anything contrary. John 8:31-32 says, ''You shall know my word which is the truth and the truth shall set you free.'' His word is the only true thing, not the things which have been said or names you have been called by anyone other than Him. I guess now I know what that word from Him did to me - it FREED me. Knowing His word, what He has called me, and who I am in Him, has given me freedom.

"What has He called me?" you are probably asking.

He has called you gifted
He has called you wonderfully and beautifully made
He has called you His delight
He has called you important, a part of his Kingdom and work
He has said you are predestined to do good works
He has called you a new living being
He has called you blessed
He has said you are fiercely loved
He has called you a conqueror
He has called you powerful
He has called you spirit
He has called you worthy
He has called you victorious
He has called you strong
He has called you bold
He has said you have His mind, the mind of Christ
He has called you His child and so much more.

We ONLY NEED to pay attention and abide. Then, He will give you more new names that you were not expecting; names that come with new meanings and assignments. this, I have been privileged to witness and experience.

He will call you singer
He will call you artist
He will call your writer
He will call you teacher
He will call you friend to many
He will call you sister/brother to His children
He will call you mother and father
He will call you lover
He will call you giver
He will call you administrator
He will call you nurturer
He will call you intercessor
He will call you provider
He will call you pastor
He will call you prophet
He will call you director
He will call you actor
He will call you obedient
He will call you protector
He will call you fighter
He will call you worshipper
He will call you extrovert
He will call you fearless
He will call you pure
He will call you redeemed
He will call you discerning
He will call you wise
He will call you survivor
He will call you president
He will call you leader
He will call you important

He will call you Esther
He will call you Lydia
He will call you Sarah
He will call you Mary
He will call you dreamer
He will call you visionary
He will call you His friend and His partner.

Once He does, the names and voices of the former things you have been or are still being will go away. From then on, they will no longer be a part of you nor hold any weight, because you know who you are and what you have been called by Him who matters the most, He who gives names. Only His word will remain which is the truth that frees us. It is my prayer that you receive grace to walk, claim and live in this newness, this new name because that is what He has called you.

16th December 2019

{Office canteen after reading Exodus 4:1-17 from Masterlife Book 2, Week 1, Day 3}

WHAT IS DOUBT?

৵৽৶

Are we not all so fortunate that we serve a patient God?

I just read Exodus 4, specifically 1-17 where God sends Moses out on an assignment, but it just seems like Moses is so quick to throw excuse after excuse. I think he does this out of doubt and fear of being let down or embarrassed in front of those God has sent him to. At first, Moses is afraid that they (the people of the world) will not believe him or that he was sent by God. To help Moses, God performs four miracles right in front of his eyes and goes on to instruct him. Moses then goes on to question his own ability to carry the instruction out due to his speech impediments and lack of eloquence. God simply responds by asking Moses "Who made man's mouth? Is it not I the Lord?"

I took this in and was completely triggered on so many levels, one being the relatability of this story. I was instantly reminded of how we fall into disobedience because we place our own opinions above His instructions. Didn't Moses realize who created him and even these men he was so afraid to meet in the first place?

Are we stepping out of God's will and purpose for our lives because we are so preoccupied with our own 'imperfections' and 'opinions' and using them to disqualify ourselves? Is that why we do not even understand that it's for those specific reasons we may have been called in the first place?

What's worse, is that we then forget that He who has called us, is He who created us, gives life, performs miracles and qualifies the unqualified according to His will and great purpose.

Disqualifying yourself because you believe you are not able to, for whatsoever reason is a form of disobedience, lack of faith and furthermore pride.

What makes you think you are not good enough?

Why do you think you get a choice in determining your own qualification apart from He who has sent you?

You only doubt and are afraid when you do not fully trust, so are you saying you do not trust or have enough faith in Me? Then why do you ask and say you want to know or fulfil purpose, do you have enough faith to humble yourself; to trust me, to go when I say go; to wait when I say wait; to speak when I say speak; to leave when I say leave; do when I say do?

Lest not forget also, that even when we see ourselves as qualified or over qualified because some of us are naturally gifted or able to, that we can do nothing of our own accords anyways, He is the one who allows, who gives power, who gives strength, who gives talents, who gives direction and the capacity to do His will.

7th January 2020

{Day 2 of a fast with the Ignite team; reading Matthew 9:16-17}

A MISMATCH

அ~ஓ

The Message Version words it differently in a way that just breaks it down and says it all truly. "No one cuts up a fine silk scarf to patch old work clothes; you want fabrics that match. And you do not put your wine in cracked bottles."

As a believer in this world, we are at a crossroads. We all face a daily battle; well, I do. As I meditated on this scripture, I had a major light bulb moment that raised questions like:

Why did I often feel off?
Why were there disconnects at certain times?
Why did I feel like a fraud sometimes?
Why was I at a crossroads or stuck in between?
Why was there no growth or why was it slow?
Why did I struggle with my identity?

The simple answer I just received in this moment was because there still was a mismatch. You cannot merge something that is dead to something that has just received newness of life. Have you ever heard the phrase you cannot outwork a bad diet? Well, it is pretty much the same thing here because you cannot integrate the old, dead you to a new life and expect it to work. Certain things just should not and do not go together. In this case, your old life of sin and this new life in Christ. Your old lifestyle, habits, past influences, personality traits; in some case, some relationships, friendships, jobs, businesses, ambitions just do not match this new life. It is a losing game to try to fit the two together, I will personally tell you that. It is a harsh reality but the truth of what it is to be transformed and reborn.

The rebirth is so that there is now a match in every area that will bring about preservation rather than a wear and tear; the latter is what happens when there is a mismatch. No matter how long or hard you try, it cannot work. In the long run, one will have to give and often it is the new.

We cannot afford to hold on to the old to truly live and survive, a rebirth is eminent for the perfect match.

God, I have tried to manage the old and the new but today I come humbly to you to say that it does not work, and to be honest, I am tired of trying to balance both. It is like the more I try to hold on to the old to still fit into the world and get along with people as I once did, the more I feel like I am giving up parts of the new and part of you. I don't want to do that anymore, I don't want to let go of an inch of this new life you have given me, this new love, this new relationship, this new communion, this new friendship, this new partnership, this new accessibility, this new me in You. So, I'm asking that you help me. I have experienced and believe in your transformative and redemptive nature and I desire a renewal, a restoration, a rebirth and its unveiling more than ever.

Lord let it start with me; give me strength and the willingness to burn bridges so I cannot return just like Elisha. Give me the courage to boldly leap into this new life completely; open up my heart and fill me up with more of You so I can go on a deeper walk. Help me to see that I will not be losing anything but only gaining and regaining. Help me to no longer care about the things of the world or need its validations, just Yours. Help keep me centred and focused on You.

Help and teach me to have a heart that consistently and fearlessly chases after You; transform me from within and let Your unveiling be done.

26th January 2020

{Psalm 66:12 - 'You let men ride over our heads; we went through fire and through water; yet you have brought us out to a place of abundance'}

A REMINDER

Today, I'm reminded of the fires and the floods
Of the trials and tests
Of the attacks and battles
Of the tears and hardships
Of the hell and strongholds.
Today, I am reminded of how loyal in Your love you are,
      And it led me to the question, can we ever praise You enough?
I am reminded of how You held my hand through it all
I am reminded of how You showed me it would be well
I am reminded of how You defended as men tried to trample over me
I am reminded of the promises that You have kept
I am reminded that, that which I thought was punishment or just non-stop trials were a setup
I am reminded that in those seasons You were refining, and pruning
I am reminded of all the things You shielded me from, known and unknown
I am reminded that You always bring us out of those same fire and flood
I am reminded of Your works
I am reminded that You are the same God that parted the way for your children to walk by foot on deep waters
I am reminded of all what You have done
I am reminded that You have done it over and over again

I am reminded of how mindful You are of me
I am reminded that because of You, I have not been caught slipping
I am reminded that You are never caught unawares
I am reminded of Your willingness
I am reminded that You allow for a reason
I am reminded that Your revelation of the whys is bigger than those
seasons
I am reminded of where I am now compared to where I once was
I am reminded of Your wonders
I am also reminded that You don't owe me any of these things but yet
here I am
Today, I am reminded of Your faithfulness,
And of Your love.
Most importantly, of how worthy You are of my praise, all the glory,
every worship and much more.

I am reminded with such urgency again why I am to carry and lift You up with pride, why Your name and praise should never be away from my tongue, why Your children should experience You through me, why they should hear about You through me, why Your name should always be blessed.

Praise to Your name should be limitless.
It should never be enough.
No one deserves all the glory like You do.

All my worship just seems to always fall short because You truly are worthy of it all and then some more.

Trumpets, harps, marching bands, Songs of praises, dancing till we can't feel our feet, bows, hands lifted high, bursts of jubilation, shouts of victory, falling on knees ....till we feel like we are out of body, even that wouldn't scratch the surface. All acts of worship as an attempt to express the magnitude of what You have done and who You are in our lives. There has never and there will never be anything like it. Today, I am reminded that neither words nor all my worship will ever be enough.

27th March 2020

THE POWER OF YOUR LOVE

The power of Your love is endless.
Pour out Your love on me, so I do not stay the same.
Only Your love can move me
Only Your love can save me
Only Your love can redeem me
Only Your love can refine me
Only Your love can transform my heart
Only Your love can give me a renewed mind
Only Your love can revive my spirit
Only Your love can heal me
Only Your love can satisfy me
Only Your love can erase my past
Only Your love can give me a future
Only Your love can override every lie
Only Your love can take away the pain
Only Your love can make me whole again
Only Your love can make me love like you do
Only Your love can make me pursue you with my all
Only Your love can help me remain
*Only Your love can make me better; a better friend, sister, daughter,
steward, employee, mother, partner, employer*
Only in Your love can my identity be found
Only Your love has allowed my heart to find perfect peace
Only Your love can reawaken dry bones
Only Your love can empower me to say No More.

To you again, dear reader

I hope this helps.

I hope this lets you know you're not alone.

I hope this reassures you.

I hope there's a fire that's been reignited again.

I hope you're filled with passion like you once were.

I hope you feel like there's hope again.

I hope you understand no one really has it all together, we're all just taking steps forward and trying every day.

I hope you understand it's not easy and it's costly but it's worth it.

I hope you were able to feel the love that I experience and know that you also have access to that love.

I hope this helps you take one more step towards surrender.

I hope you were able to relate with me even just a smidge.

I hope you're open to let yourself go through the healing process.

I hope you want to be the real deal.

I hope you have a new desire to yield.

I hope you're yearning for a deeper connection.

I hope you want your own back and forth with Him.

I hope you desire such a friendship.

I hope new gifts and interests are ignited.

I hope your heart is on fire for Him like never before.

I hope you're thirsty for maturity in your relationship.

11th April 2020

Today, I declare to the Lord that I will dwell, that I will tarry. I declare that I will finally stop running, stop fussing, stop fighting but sit still. I declare today that I cease from my works and enter into Your rest.

I declare that from this moment on, I have returned to my position of worship at His feet where I will stay forever, where my request for His presence will be my greatest need. Where He will be my only option, where there will be complete trust and surrender. Where my eyes will be fixed on Him as I let every other thing fade away.

MY NAME IS DAMMY FEYIDE, HEPHZIBAH – HIS DELIGHT, HIS MASTERPIECE AND LET IT BE KNOWN NOW AND FOREVER THAT I BELONG COMPLETELY TO YOU & I AM A WOMAN WHO PURSUES YOU LORD, WITH ALL HER HEART.

ACKNOWLEDGEMENTS

ॐॐ

Whoooosh! What a whirlwind and what a year it has been. Thank you to every single person, named and unnamed who has been on this journey with me this year till this point, in one way or the other.

Thank you, Dad, for everything. I am always so grateful.

Thank you, my beautiful angel of a mother, words will never be enough truly.

To Femi, Moyo and Tammy- Thank you for teaching me how to love, for letting me love you and for loving me.

Thank you Derin for being there as the first person I told about this, for reading every draft at every stage, for every feedback, for the phone calls that became only about this. Thank you for being my person, for being the Christina Yang to my Meredith Grey (without the exit).

Thank you my Mazino, for allowing God use you as the starting point of my journey, as someone that I could relate with. Thank you for your patience and consistency, for answering the questions I had, for letting me go on my own journey but not being far away. Thank you for letting me read out entries to you, thank you for calling me a writer even when I did not see it, thank you for the book club we started to proofread this book, thank you for enduring the times I was physically present but absent from bonding times because I was writing or working on this. I honor your entire family, my other siblings Orezimena and Maro. A big shout out to Mind County for the space you have created.

To my sister Tamara - There is nothing in my life that you are not a part or a witness of and this is clear proof of that. Thank you for being my person, for being proof that as you accept and receive

Gods' love he pours out and surrounds you with the best of the best. For teaching me the true meaning of openness and unconditional love in a friendship. You read and gave me the first feedback. Asides becoming sisters, we have become partners over the past year in more ways than one. I honour you #maskoffforever.

Pastor Bisola, my mum - Thank you for letting me be the adult child you did not ask for but got. For every incoming call you received, and for trusting me and seeing me. Thank you for letting me know that there was more to me, for all that you called me, for raising me, for the prayer calls or random check ins, for reading this even during all you have going on, for bringing me into Ignite, for helping me find my place and so much more.

To my TTWJ family, thank you for being home to me. This was the first space I ever read out anything I had ever written and what that started in me, you will never know. You saw this even before I did, and so did my Masterlife family, for the 'Oh, do you have a writing blog?' and 'Oh, are you a writer?' comments. Thank you for what you ignited in me.

To my Ignite army, thank you for being a family behind me.

To Ore Oshin, Fola Olowu & Oyin Oshiafi my listeners and strategists. We are so different but so perfect together. It just works with you 3 individually and is the sweetest thing. Thank you for the long calls and rants and research and reminding me i could do this my Oreo. Thank you for always being my right hand, reminding me I can rely on you and always thinking ahead for me Oyin. Thank you my Folly, for being my fighter, for asking me the tough questions, for direction, for reading even when we both know your not a book person lool, for not giving up on me/us. Folly, there was a moment there when i was crawling back to hide but in your own fashion you said exactly what I needed.

My sisters & Tribe; Dara (for all the tears loool my feedback queen), Yetunde (Tictac), Naomi, Ugonna, My Janjan, Cynthia, Dolapo O, Tenikins, Suni Agwaeze, Osoba and last but not the least David U Ole (Thank you for saying Yes and partnering with me on this, the new ideas you gave me, wisdom and vision you shared with me and fro seeing this even before I did). I honour you all for your time, words and the love you have for me that has taught me so much.

To every single person who has contributed to getting me here and been there this past year. There is a lot of sweetness, wisdom, encouragement that has been poured into me through you individually. I acknowledge and honour you all.

To PA and Omotayo Adeola, forewords will never be the same after these words. I honour you both.

To Omotayo Adeola, fire catcher and my helper along this journey. It started with a frantic DM because I wasn't sure how I got to write a manuscript. 'Thank you' will never be enough. For what you saw, for what you called it, for ALL the texts and calls, for the direction, for pointing me to the right people, for editing for me, for formatting with me, for bringing out the artist in me, for turning what I scribbled down at Nuli to my book cover, for the genius you brought, for your vulnerability, for letting me know I could do this and that I didn't need what I thought I needed, for reading every updated version and the list goes on.

Thank you, Sharon of Stratum Pages for being you and being on this journey with me. Thank you for something you said that confirmed something God was trying to say to me. Thank you for this new friendship.

Thank you Emeka Ogey and Free State Publishing for believing in me and in this, for all the time, encouragement and advice.

Thank you, Femi & Expand Press Limited Team, for all

your patience and work on bringing this project together. For all the calls, back and forth, listening to me, understanding what this is and bringing it to life. I am so grateful to you and your team.

To Eva Akaabar (Levi online publishing), Thank you so much for your excellence. For making this process such smooth sailing and helping me with the heavy final lifting.

Finally! To my main Guy, words will never be enough but I Thank You and I Behold you ABBA. From beginning to the end it has and always will be you, we did this & all this for your Glory!

ABOUT THE BOOK

Hephzibah's Anthology is a heart conversation that talks about the trials of life and overcoming them through faith. Anyone who has ever felt lost and broken and is seeking a way to redemption will instantly connect with the words in the book.

It is a collection of intimate conversations between the author and her Maker and it will take you on a journey of self-discovery that will have you laughing, crying but most importantly, reflecting deeply. It will make you question man's purpose in life while reminding you of God's bigger plan.

ABOUT THE AUTHOR

৵৹

Dammy Feyide is the wordsmith behind *Hephzibah's Anthology*. She works in Strategy and Business Intelligence at a bank in Nigeria. She graduated with a degree in Economics and Business Management from the University of Sheffield, UK. She is a qualified personal trainer, a writer, poet, a business owner and lover of alternative/indie rock music.

She is passionate about equipping women and building communities, as well as the work she does in developing kids through her School of Arts programme in collaboration with her partner NGO. She is a foodie, obsessed with her family and friends, loves dogs, is a big softie contrary to what she portrays externally.

She hopes to one day live by the beach where she will get to walk around bare-footed while falling asleep to the sounds of the ocean.'